She's Deeply Rooted

An Inspirational & Interactive Journal

Haydee Irving

YAH-Scribe Publishing

Contents

Copyrights	V
Letter From the Publisher	VI
Letter From the Editor	VIII
Introduction	X
1. We Need A Savior	1
2. The Gift	5
3. Holy Spirit, Help	11
4. Let Me Testify	17
5. Get Rid of It	22
6. Perseverance	26
7. Insulting Grace	29
8. Stop The Search	32
9. Who Can I Run To?	35
10. Family	38
11. Parents	44

12. Return to your Lane	47
13. Let's Stop Pretending	50
14. Your Addiction Is Killing You	53
15. Sarah, Girl...	56
16. Letting Him Uproot	60
17. This Is Your Reminder...	63
18. Broken Church System	65
Afterword	68
Photosynthesis Bible Study Template	
About the Author	80

Copyright © 2024 by Haydee Irving

All rights reserved.

No portion of this book may be reproduced in any form without written permission from the publisher or author, except as permitted by U.S. copyright law.

This publication is designed to provide accurate and authoritative information in regard to the subject matter covered. It is sold with the understanding that neither the author nor the publisher is engaged in rendering legal, investment, accounting or other professional services. While the publisher and author have used their best efforts in preparing this book, they make no representations or warranties with respect to the accuracy or completeness of the contents of this book and specifically disclaim any implied warranties of merchantability or fitness for a particular purpose. No warranty may be created or extended by sales representatives or written sales materials. The advice and strategies contained herein may not be suitable for your situation. You should consult with a professional when appropriate. Neither the publisher nor the author shall be liable for any loss of profit or any other commercial damages, including but not limited to special, incidental, consequential, personal, or other damages.

Book Cover: by Blaine Irving

Editor: Aleah M'Poko

Letter From the Publisher

BY BLAINE IRVING

My Darling Haydee,

Happy, happy birthday to you on your very special day.

Every year, your birthday turns out a bit differently. Some years, I have known what to do for you, while other years, I haven't had a clue. Earlier this year (about 6 months before your birthday), God spoke to me about taking everything you have written and will continue to write for His glory and turning it into a book. Today, as you look through this book, you will see the fullness of the fruit of your labor and obedience to God. People worldwide have been blessed by your obedience and your sacrifice as you have meticulously studied and spent time with the Spirit of God to teach His people on a weekly basis. Your time and dedication have uplifted, encouraged, and empowered people in the Spirit to become better versions of themselves daily.

I so look forward to seeing what God is going to do for you and for the people through this book as you continue to be the influence He called you to be as a leader for His Kingdom.

I hope you enjoy this book with your name on it. It has been the hardest thing in the world to keep this a secret until your birthday. I am so proud of you for becoming an author for the second time.

Continue letting Him use you for His glory.

All my love.

Your hubby,
— Blaine

Letter From the Editor

By Aleah M'Poko

Father God, I thank You for Haydee—a dear friend and sister in Christ. Thank You for her love. Thank You for her generosity, and her friendship, and her faithfulness to You, and her wisdom, and her curiosity. Thank You for her gift for teaching and worshipping and understanding Your word and Your ways. Thank You for her vulnerability. Thank You for her obedience. Thank You for her example. Thank you for the fruit of her womb. Thank You that, before the foundation of the earth, You ordained my friendship with her. Thank You for letting me experience her and share Your love with her. I pray she has an unshakeable knowing of how much she means to those around her.

I pray that You give her peace, LORD. Help her to lean on and hope confidently in You, that Your perfect peace may prevail in her life. Give her the strength to endure every trial You allow and the wisdom and discernment to navigate them. May she continue to trust in You with all her heart and lean not on her own understanding. May she acknowledge You in all her ways that You may direct her path. May she seek You above all else and hide herself in Your word. May she remember Your goodness every moment of every day and prioritize Your will over her own. May she be acutely aware of Your presence as she goes through her day—every day—and may she embody the fruit of Your Spirit that others may experience You through her.

Help her to be all that You desire for her to be. Quiet her with Your love. Keep her hunger and thirst for Your righteousness alive. Help her choose life, every moment of every day. Help her to meet You in the present moment. Remind her that as one who loves You and is called according to Your purpose, all things are surely working together for her good. Thank You for all that You've made her to be, LORD. Help her to love and be that person. It's in the precious name of Your Son, Jesus Christ, that I ask these things. Amen.

Haydee, it's an honor to be able to witness what God is doing in and through you. What a blessing to have been a part of this special project that has ministered to me in the process.

Love you, lady.

Introduction

Welcome to She's Deeply Rooted, a community purposed to bring you closer to God. In 2019, I was in an odd place: recently married, pregnant with our second, and greatly lacking community. I felt so far from God, trying to multitask in my multiple roles, until I hit a roadblock and asked God, "Why am I here? This feels lonely."

In 2015, when I accepted Jesus, I gave everything up and began to experience a deep loneliness. But I didn't dwell on it because I was so focused on God and trying to be healed that I didn't take time to process the root of it. I saw God deliver me from homosexuality, being a pothead, a drunk, a liar, a gossiper, a fornicator, and so much more. But there I was, 4 years later, struggling and feeling stagnant in my relationship with God.

I would pray and cry out to God, asking Him to deliver me from the loneliness—to set me free from this stagnation I was feeling. He answered me gently, telling me to "go deeper." I was like, "Huh?" Lol. "Uh... God, I pray, worship, and yes, I may be a little distracted here and there, but what do you mean "go deeper"?"

I began to hear "She's Deeply Rooted" over and over again, and I decided to launch a podcast named SDR. It failed because I wasn't deeply rooted in Him. I was still struggling with fear of people's opinions, questioning whether I heard God or not, and paranoid that people were going to hurt me. On top of that, I didn't feel like a good wife, and I felt like a horrible mother. All of this made me feel alone.

I realized that I needed to dig deeper in God. So I went on a journey to draw closer to Him, studying to make sure I knew what I believed in and detoxing from popular Christian preachers/celebrities. I began to test every spirit, and it came down to relying solely on God, His word, and the Holy Spirit. I discovered that the reason I felt alone was because I wasn't rooted in who God had designed me to be as His daughter. I was so focused on trying to be what everyone else thought I should be that I forgot who I belonged to and shifted.

I began to pray dangerously by faith, believing for the intangible things—boldness, peace, joy, conviction, more of Him and less of me. I prayed for my flesh to die, for His wisdom, to worship Him in Spirit and in truth, for fear of His glory, but most importantly, His will. Through this, I began to grow in Him.

I realized that the more rooted in Him I became, the freer I would live. I have only one mission, and that's to spread His gospel. I desire for other women to grow deeper in God and experience the same freedom so we can truly bring light into this world. We have been slaves to the world long enough; it's time to come into agreement with His Spirit and do His will on earth as it is in Heaven.

It's 2024, and you have been selected to live in this time. The enemy has been trying to take you out since birth, but he lost, and you are here to fulfill the will of your Father, who desires for you to be whole in Him. Let's start the digging process.

Chapter One
We Need A Savior

Savior: [noun] a person who saves someone or something from danger and who is regarded with the veneration of a religious figure; God or Jesus Christ as the redeemer of sin and saver of souls
— I appreciate that the dictionary acknowledges our savior as Jesus Christ.

Veneration: [noun] great respect; reverence (fear of the Lord)

Why Do We Need a Savior?
Because we are ghetttoooo. Our first nature isn't always to do the right thing. We are selfish, rotten, and it can be hard to change that, BUT there is One who can wash us clean: Jesus. HALLELUJAH. Can you imagine living in a world filled with evil and having no way out? No hope? That sounds horrible...

We should be thankful for the shedding of His blood and the freedom it bought for us—thank You, Lord, for the shedding of Your blood. We need a savior because we live in a fallen world that has nurtured us into some evil, wicked people. I know that may sound harsh, but it's the truth. And the truth will set us free the moment we have a reality check with ourselves that humbles and changes our heart posture. It is at this point that we realize we were dead all along. And dead people can only produce dead things. But through Jesus, we come alive, and with the gift of the Holy Spirit, we can produce good fruit.

John 14:6 *"Jesus answered, "I am the way and the truth and the life. No one comes to the Father except through me.""* (NIV)

Revelation 1:5 *"and from Jesus Christ, who is the faithful witness, the firstborn from the dead, and the ruler of the kings of the earth. To him who loves us and has freed us from our sins by his blood,"* (NIV)

Why Is Jesus Your Savior?
If you do not get passionate by answering this question, then you need to dig deeper.

Jesus is my Savior because He saved me from myself. He saved me from danger. He saved me from sexual abuse, sexual immorality, anger, witchcraft, promiscuity, insecurities, drug abuse, alcoholism, and so much more. He came to save me at the lowest point in my life when I felt like I had no purpose—like I had nothing to live for and I was useless. He redeemed me, at which point there was no denying that Jesus is God. A fear of the Lord rose inside of me, and I couldn't turn back.

SHARE YOUR TESTIMONY

My desire is that you don't take this section lightly, but that you receive it with urgency. The enemy has been trying to shut your mouth and keep you away from sharing your testimony of Jesus because he knows the power it holds. In the book of Acts, souls were getting saved by the testimonies of Jesus. They heard and saw the evidence of Jesus touching peoples' lives. Jesus had to tell some people to be quiet about the miracles He had performed in their lives because it wasn't time for people to know yet. I believe that Jesus knew the power of our words—that they can create a spreading fire that cannot be contained.

Do not allow the enemy to place shame or fear on you, for you are truly saved from danger through Jesus Christ:

Isaiah 54:4-5 *"Do not be afraid; you will not be put to shame. Do not fear disgrace; you will not be humiliated. You will forget the shame of your youth and remember no more the reproach of your widowhood. For your Maker is your husband—the Lord Almighty is his name—the Holy One of Israel is your Redeemer; he is called the God of all the earth."* (NIV)

You do not need a platform to share your testimony. *You* are the platform and microphone. Help the captives be set free:

Isaiah 61:1 *"The Spirit of the Sovereign Lord is on me, because the Lord has anointed me to proclaim good news to the poor. He has sent me to bind up the brokenhearted, to proclaim freedom for the captives and release from darkness for the prisoners,"* (NIV)

Depression, anxiety, sexual immorality, murder, anger, pride, and other evil things are taking souls every day. The kingdom of heaven should be taking double souls. And so it shall. You've been trying to figure out your purpose on earth and this right here is your purpose:

Matthew 28: 19-20 *"Therefore go and make disciples of all nations, baptizing them in the name of the Father and of the Son and of the Holy Spirit, and teaching them to obey everything I have commanded you. And surely I am with you always, to the very end of the age."* (NIV) — A command from the mouth of Jesus.

Open up your mouth, use your hands to type or sign, and use your feet to walk and spread the gospel through your testimony.

Let Us Pray

God, I thank You for saving us. I thank You for delivering us from the danger. God, I ask that You give us the boldness to share Your gospel—the Good News. Give us the courage, God. You did not give us a spirit of fear but of power, love, and a sound mind. God, thank You for taking our shame away on the cross. We love You, Lord, and we know You are with us as we go forth. In Jesus' name, we pray. Amen.

> **CHALLENGE FOR THE WEEK**
> Share your testimony with one person this week. You can share how He saved you, how He healed you, or a miracle He performed in Your life.

Chapter Two
The Gift

I have gone through a roller coaster learning about **the Gift** and understanding that we truly do not understand His function. Jesus let us know this would happen... Because it requires us to accept and receive **the Gift** to understand Him. The church stops at Jesus, but Jesus didn't stop with just Himself. He said there was One coming after Him, and during His time on earth, He showed us how, why, and when it would happen.

If *fear* stops you from learning about **the Gift,** understand that **the spirit of fear is evil** and **should not reside in your temple**. You have the authority to fight that temptation—not just with the name of Jesus, but also through **the Gift**—and the enemy knows this, so he tries to keep you from the truth. As you continue reading, I pray that the spirit of understanding falls on you so that you may have clarity and receive **the Gift**.

A LOT OF SCRIPTURE IS BEING PROVIDED BELOW SO THAT YOU CAN SEE WHAT THE BIBLE SAYS, NOT SOMETHING THAT HAYDEE CAME UP WITH. LOL

Gift: [noun] a thing given willingly to someone without payment; a natural ability or talent

Genesis 1:1-2 *"In the beginning God created the heavens and the earth. Now the earth was formless and empty, darkness was over the surface of the deep, and the* **Spirit of God** *was hovering over the waters."* (NIV)

The Gift AKA **The Spirit of God** AKA **The Holy Spirit** AKA **The Advocate** has been here since the beginning; it (He) hovered over the earth. The Holy Spirit was with God in the process of creation. Jesus was there too (John 1:1).

Genesis 1:26 *"Then God said,* **"Let us make mankind in our image***, in our likeness, so that they may rule over the fish in the sea and the birds in the sky, over the livestock and all the wild animals, and over all the creatures that move along the ground.""* (NIV)

This confirms that God is three in one. He is God our Father, God the Son, and God the Holy Spirit.

How Did Jesus Exemplify The Power of the Holy Spirit?

Matthew 3:13-17 *"Then Jesus came from Galilee to the Jordan to be baptized by John. But John tried to deter him, saying, "I need to be baptized by you, and do you come to me?" Jesus replied,* **"Let it be so now; it is proper for us to do this to fulfill all righteousness."** *Then John consented.* ***As soon as Jesus was baptized, he went up out of the water. At that moment heaven was opened, and he saw the Spirit of God descending***

like a dove and alighting on him. And a voice from heaven said, "This is my Son, whom I love; with him I am well pleased."" (NIV)

Luke 3:21-22 *"When all the people were being baptized, Jesus was baptized too. And as he was praying, heaven was opened and the Holy Spirit descended on him in bodily form like a dove. And a voice came from heaven: "You are my Son, whom I love; with you I am well pleased."* (NIV)

To fulfill righteousness, Jesus needed to be baptized and receive the Spirit of God. They created everything together, saved us together, and functioned together. Also, I find it interesting that **God the Father, God the Son, and God the Holy Spirit** are written about in Chapter **3** of both books. Super random, but powerful.

Another example of the power of the Holy Spirit happened right after Jesus was baptized.

Matthew 4:1-11 *"Then Jesus was led by the Spirit into the wilderness to be tempted by the devil. After fasting forty days and forty nights, he was hungry. The tempter came to him and said, "If you are the Son of God, tell these stones to become bread." Jesus answered, "It is written: 'Man shall not live on bread alone, but on every word that comes from the mouth of God.'" Then the devil took him to the holy city and had him stand on the highest point of the temple. "If you are the Son of God," he said, "throw yourself down. For it is written: "'He will command his angels concerning you, and they will lift you up in their hands, so that you will not strike your foot against a stone.'" Jesus answered him, "It is also written: 'Do not put the Lord your God to the test.'" Again, the devil took him to a very high mountain and showed him all the kingdoms of the world and their splendor. "All this I will give you," he said, "if you will bow down and worship me." Jesus said to* *him, "Away from me, Satan! For it is written: 'Worship the Lord your God, and serve him only.'" Then the devil left him, and angels came and attended him."* (NIV)

Matthew 4:17 *"From that time on Jesus began to preach, "Repent, for the kingdom of heaven has come near.""* (NIV)

The Holy Spirit led Jesus into the wilderness; He did not lead Jesus into temptation, just for clarity (1 Corinthians 10:13). In the wilderness, after fasting for 40 days and 40 nights (whew, chile I can't even.. lol) Jesus was tempted by the devil. Why do we fast? So that our flesh can die and the Holy Spirit can be at the forefront. Jesus was able to show the fruit of the Holy Spirit as He beat up the devil with the Spirit of **truth**, causing the enemy to flee as the angels came to assist Him. At last, after killing the flesh and allowing the Spirit of Truth (AKA Holy Spirit) to flow, Jesus was able to come out of the wilderness and begin His ministry. He seriously went through a human experience to set us free. Not only did He take us in; He taught us what we would be doing after His salvation and through the Holy Spirit.

Why Do We Need the Holy Spirit?

- Because Jesus had The Holy Spirit and because He said so lol.

John 15:26-27 *"When the Advocate comes, whom I will send to you from the Father—the Spirit of truth who goes out from the Father—he will testify about me. And you also must testify, for you have been with me from the beginning."* (NIV)

John 16: 7-15 *"But very truly I tell you, it is for your good that I am going away. Unless I go away, the Advocate will not come to you; but if I go, I will send him to you. When he comes, he will prove the world to be in the wrong about sin and righteousness and judgment: about sin, because people do not believe in me; about righteousness, because I am going to the Father, where you can see me no longer; and about judgment, because the prince of this world now stands condemned. I have much more to say to you, more than you can now bear. But when he, the Spirit of truth, comes, he will guide you into all the truth. He will not speak on his own; he will speak only what he hears, and he will tell you what is yet to come. He will glorify me because it is from me that he will receive what he will make known to you. All that belongs to the Father is mine. That is why I said the Spirit will receive from me what he will make known to you."* (NIV)

Jesus gave us a powerful gift for free and we need to start acknowledging Him. There are so many things that our human mind cannot comprehend because of our flesh, but those mysteries can be revealed through the Holy Spirit. That is how we begin to understand the spiritual realm (Ephesians 6:12). We begin to understand the realm we should be operating from: The Kingdom. He comes alive, the Bible comes alive, we come alive. We cannot truly experience the fullness of God without <u>all</u> of Him— which is God the Father, God the Son, and God The Holy Spirit. And we can see that in all of this, WE NEED THE HOLY SPIRIT. He completes the God in us (which brings me to my last point).

He Unifies the Body of Christ. He Unifies His Bride.

Acts 2:1-4 *"When the day of Pentecost came, they were all together in one place. Suddenly a sound like the blowing of a violent wind came from heaven* *and filled the whole house where they were sitting. They saw what seemed to be tongues of fire that separated and came to rest on each of them. All of them were filled with the Holy Spirit and began to speak in other tongues as the Spirit enabled them."* (NIV)

This is just one example of the mystery and unity of the Holy Spirit. Continue reading the book of Acts to see the rest. As you get stirred, you will want the Holy Spirit because you will see something you don't see in the church today: **THE POWER OF THE HOLY SPIRIT**.

Chapter Three
Holy Spirit, Help

Alright, I know I've been giving you all a lot of scripture. And that's because there is no way for us to grow in God without knowing His word. You cannot base your relationship with God on what someone else says or what they think the Bible says. You need to be confident and clear in who you believe in, especially as you get tested in your faith walk.

In Chapter 2, we learned about The Holy Spirit. We learned that He was a gift given to us through the death and resurrection of Jesus Christ. **The way to receive this gift is through repentance and baptism (Acts 2:38).** I think a lot of people struggle to understand repentance because they relate it to condemnation and it triggers their pride/trauma. But repentance brings freedom. Let me give you a vision of how I see repentance: Imagine someone throwing cold water at you on a hot summer day. At first, it's shockingly cold, but then it becomes refreshing and you experience relief from the heat.

Acts 3:19 *"Repent, then, and turn to God, so that your sins may be wiped out, that times of refreshing may come from the Lord"* (NIV)

Romans 8:1-4 *"Therefore, there is now no condemnation for those who are in Christ Jesus, <u>because through Christ Jesus the law of the Spirit who gives life has set you free from the law of sin and death</u>. For what the <u>law was powerless to do because it was weakened by the flesh, God did by sending his own Son in the likeness of sinful flesh to be a sin offering</u>. And so he condemned sin in the flesh, in order that the righteous requirement of the law might be fully met in us, who do not live according to the flesh but according to the Spirit."* (NIV) — Please meditate on this scripture and continue reading this chapter. It's powerful!

Repent: [verb] feel or express sincere regret or remorse about one's wrongdoing or sin

- *__Hebrew: to turn and go a different direction__*

- *__Greek: to change one's mindset__*

Romans 1:18-19 *"The wrath of God is being revealed from heaven against all the godlessness and wickedness of people, who suppress the truth by their wickedness, since what may be known about God is plain to them, because God has made it plain to them."* (NIV)

Repentance requires humility and receiving the knowledge that you are a sinner. You acknowledge that you are a wicked person. Now when people hear the word "wicked" they tend to gasp in disbelief because they don't see themselves that way. People generally see themselves as good people. But truthfully, we don't know what "good" is because our definition of good has been distorted through our sinful nature. But God's goodness cannot be compared to our definition, because His goodness is **holy**, which we are not. That's why we need to accept the **Holy Spirit**. *The*

Holy Spirit leads us to holiness.

<u>Holy Spirit:</u> God is *spiritually active* in the world. In Hebrew, it is called Ruach Ha-Kodesh

<u>Ruach:</u> The word *ruach* intially meant "wind," but later came to refer to the whole range of a *person's emotional, intellectual, and volitional life.*

<u>Ha-Kodesh:</u> The Spirit of the Holy One

1 Corinthians 6:15-20 *"Do you not know that your bodies are members of Christ himself? Shall I then take the members of Christ and unite them with a prostitute? Never! Do you not know that he who unites himself with a prostitute is one with her in body? For it is said, "The two will become one flesh." But whoever is united with the Lord is one with him in spirit. Flee from sexual immorality. All other sins a person commits are outside the body, but whoever sins sexually, sins against their own body. Do you not know that your bodies are temples of the Holy Spirit, who is in you, whom you have received from God? You are not your own; you were bought at a price. Therefore honor God with your bodies."* (NIV) — I know this scripture mentions sexual immorality, but it applies to any sin that separates you from God.

After you get baptized, repent, and receive the Holy Spirit, your life changes because it no longer belongs to you. Your body becomes a construction site for the Holy Spirit. A big sign goes up on your body that says **"Holy Spirit's Temple Coming Soon."** You and the Holy Spirit team up to construct this temple. But not just any temple; a **Holy Temple** which requires breaking ground to build a new thing—a new foundation. The process gets ugly at first because you get exposed to all your ugly habits, your lifestyle, the way you talk, and even the way you think. The Holy

Spirit doesn't care how sloppy your situation is, He will come in and purify it. How? He convicts, exposes the root of the problem, extracts, and replaces it with His fruit **(Galatians 5:19-26)**.

Another example: Have you heard of a Crime Scene Cleaner? Once a crime scene has occurred, they call up a person to clean up the crime scene: the cleaner. The cleaner cleans up so well that the scene is left like nothing ever happened there. The crime scene cleaners have to inspect their work and be very detailed in what they do. The Holy Spirit is like the cleaner, but greater because His work doesn't leave any residue behind. So much so that He makes sure there is nothing left in your DNA—no trace left—of what was keeping you captive. But it doesn't end there! He makes a new covenant with you that nothing from your old life will transfer to your children or future generations in your bloodline. HALLELUJAH! **(Acts 2:39)**

How Do We Allow the Holy Spirit to Work?

- **We team up by killing our flesh. Get rid of distractions (social media, porn, people, etc.), fast (from food), and get in the word of God!**

What you were taught and what you thought you were goes completely out the window. Now you begin to transform into a new creature. *You become a son/daughter of God—free.* But you have to believe it **(Romans 8:14-17)**. Because when you want to watch pornography before going to bed or masturbating, you have to remember to say "NOOO!" When you want to gossip about your friends and how messed up their lives are to your other "Christian" friends, you have to say "NOOO!" When you want to cheat on your boyfriend/girlfriend because you need constant attention at all times, you have to say "NOOO!" When you want to sleep with multiple people because you have a sex addiction, you have to say "NOOO!" When you want to smoke and drink to run away from life, you have to say "NOOO!" When you struggle with your identity and want to seek it in other people and things, you have to say "NOOO!"

And say "HOLY SPIRIT HELP!!! ADVOCATE DELIVER ME. HEALER, HEAL ME! FLESH, DIE!"

Galatians 5:16-18 *"So I say, walk by the Spirit, and you will not gratify the desires of the flesh. For the flesh desires what is contrary to the Spirit, and the Spirit what is contrary to the flesh. They are in conflict with each other, so that you are not to do whatever you want. But if you are led by the Spirit, you are not under the law."* (NIV)

We think our biggest fight is with the devil, but our biggest fight is with our flesh. The devil only works based on access from the doors you leave open for him. But through the Holy Spirit, those doors can be SHUT with no trace left behind!

Let Us Pray

God, we acknowledge this war is not against flesh and blood, but that it's a spiritual one. And because of, this we put on the full armor You have given us: the belt of truth buckled around our waist, with the breastplate of righteousness in place, our feet fitted with the readiness that comes from the gospel of peace. We take up the shield of faith, with which we can extinguish all the flaming arrows of the evil one, we take the helmet of salvation, and the sword of the Spirit, which is the word of God. We thank You, Lord, for You are with us, in Jesus' name. Amen.

CHALLENGE FOR THE WEEK

Receive the Holy Spirit. Make a radical move and get rid of ALL distractions. If you do not know what these are, ask Holy Spirit to expose and shed light on them.

Chapter Four
Let Me Testify

My name is Blaine Irving. I grew up Christian and attended a Christian school, but I never completely understood how to have a real, intimate relationship with God. What I had been taught quickly fell apart as I grew up, and everything I had been taught about the Christian lifestyle seemed like a total façade. It sounded great in theory, but it lacked substance and practicality.

Despite all this, I still believed that God existed. I just could not understand why I never saw the manifestation of biblical-style miracles, and I often expressed to God, "Lord I want You to use me like that…" I wanted Him to use me to heal the sick and raise the dead. Yet I found it hard to comprehend that God would speak to people audibly—I struggled to wrap my head around this concept. I struggled because nothing I was being taught was manifesting around me. I didn't see people healed, and I didn't see dead people waking up. It disappointed me a bit, but I still wanted to believe it was possible.

When I turned 11 years old, my father was diagnosed with an aggressive form of lung cancer. He was given 18 months to live, but unfortunately only made it 15.5 more months. During his entire battle, I struggled with the fact that I could not stop this disease from killing him and I had an even greater struggle with the fact that no one around him—including himself—fought with enough belief that he was going to be healed. I begged God almost that entire time to heal my dad and not let him die. When he died, my heart was gutted. I was stunned. Later that same year, while I was on holiday, my mom died unexpectedly. She had been on an extended stay at the hospital with "pneumonia," but I later found out she had succumbed to lung cancer as well. I remember crying out in pain, with a scream I could not contain within the cavity of my chest. I became an orphan at the age of 11.

After losing my mom and dad, I endured several years of verbal abuse while living with family and friends. My sister eventually adopted me and I ended up moving to America with her and her new husband. This should have been a good move but the trauma I had experienced had not begun to manifest yet. As I started my early teen years, dating became a thing. I remember yearning for my own family from a very young age. With every new relationship, I dated with the intent of getting married and starting my own family.

Around the age of 16 or 17, I lost my virginity to my girlfriend at the time. Our relationship lasted for almost 2 years after this. When I was about 18, our relationship began to deteriorate and eventually ended in heartbreak. This sudden and unexpected breakup triggered a downward spiral in my emotional well-being. Up until this point, I had been very cautious about having sex outside of marriage, aside from my then-girlfriend. But after the breakup, something broke inside of me, and I started having sex with different girls—sometimes even girls I had just met the same day. With every encounter, I was breaking more and more. Despite the one-night stands and the random sexual encounters, I still longed for love and wholeness.

In 2012, at the age of 20, I traveled back to South Africa for the first time since leaving in 2005. I returned expecting people to welcome me and be loving and accepting of me as a person. But the same bondage that tried to keep me enslaved—within my family and beyond—met me once again. Throughout my life, there was this expectation of me to conform to a certain way of living, and I could never live up to it. By the end of that year, I returned to America, ready to put up my middle finger to my family and supposed friends in South Africa. I was ready to fully embrace my eccentric lifestyle. However, shortly after returning, God set me up by introducing me to someone who resembled Him.

While in South Africa, I had learned a new skill as a wedding planner, having planned over 160 weddings. It felt like I had found my purpose—something I was finally good at—but God had other plans for me. That newfound "purpose" led me to a wedding expo in Detroit, where I met a woman who happened to be Christian. She looked at me funny because of my eccentric way of dressing. I saw the judgment in her eyes, but I had become so good at deflecting peoples' arrows that I initially paid her no mind.

I was standing there when I audibly heard a voice tell me, "Buy her a ticket." I immediately knew that this voice was God. I don't know how I knew, but I did. I started arguing with Him in my head about not wanting to buy her a ticket, when all of a sudden, these words poured out of my mouth came: "God said to buy your ticket." I experienced that moment when you wish you could just grab the words and put them back in your mouth. "UGH,"

I thought. But off I went back to the box office and bought this woman's ticket.

We walked our separate ways, and I was looking at one of the last booths of the expo when I felt a tap on my shoulder. It was that same woman of God whom I had bought a ticket for. I looked up, and she immediately began to tell me what God was saying. I was stunned as she spoke about secret prayer requests that I had spoken to God about that I knew only He could have known. Requests I had made known before God began to be revealed. The accuracy and the details started to unravel my mind and my whole life began to make sense. I was different because God had created me differently.

One of the prophetic words I got that day was about who I am, how I was called to be a prophet, and the fact that God was going to use me greatly to prophesy to nations, politicians, actors, etc. I remember thinking, "I can't do that. How do you do what you do?" But the gift became fully activated that day in the presence of one of God's other prophets. Little did I know, the gift had always been inside of me. But because it had never been cultivated by anyone with an understanding of the prophetic, I never knew it existed. And on the few occasions that I inquired about something prophetic I was feeling or experiencing, others had called it witchcraft.

Over the next 3 years, God took me on a journey of growing closer to Him. A journey where He was teaching me about Himself and teaching me how to trust Him. This intensive journey was a jam-packed time of learning to understand His ways and fall in love with God Himself, not because of what He could do for me, but simply because He is good!

There were so many strongholds that were holding me captive, like finding my worth in whether my family was proud of me, or needing to prove myself as a success. I was seeking my identity and worth in things, peoples' thoughts, and societal norms. But as God continued to reveal Himself to me, I continued to be set free from the power the enemy had over me because of the curses people had spoken over me. Things I had heard throughout my life like, "You're stupid," "You're ugly," "You will never be anything," "You are gay," and "There is something wrong with you." God revealed the truth about me, that I am fearfully and wonderfully made. I am made perfectly, just the way the Creator of light wanted to make me. All I lacked up until that point was His breathtaking presence.

I cannot express enough that the first step we take in finding our true identity in God is allowing God to strip away everything that is untruth. And these are often most of the things we identify with. Sometimes we can find ourselves feeling like "OH MY GOODNESS, my whole life was a lie!" I know I sure felt that way when God first started with me.

Wow, what a powerful testimony. And I don't say this just because he is my husband, but because I have seen firsthand how God has transformed him even more from the time I met him in 2016. I pray this testimony encourages you. Make sure to share it with anyone who needs to be set free from bondage!

Follow Blaine on Instagram: @prophetblaine

Chapter Five
Get Rid of It

D*istraction: [noun] a thing that prevents someone from giving full attention to something else; extreme agitation of the mind or emotions*

Some of you are seeking a deeper relationship with God and are struggling to have that freedom to do so because of **distractions**. Distractions are so present in your life that you can't even tell when they're affecting your relationship with God. Unfortunately it's hard to see the distractions because you haven't done anything to provoke the distractions to expose themselves.

This world is filled with distractions because it was designed that way **(Ephesians 2:1-5)**. I mentioned last week that our greatest battle is with our flesh. Why is that? Because the enemy knows that he can't do anything to you unless you give him access. Distraction is one of the doors that open us up to the enemy. The enemy wants you to be unaware or clueless of the truth because knowing the truth will set you free from bondage **(Matthew 12:22-23)**.

Distractions become our "normal" because the enemy puts a cloak of false comfort over our flesh. He presents distractions that get shinier and shinier, leading us to struggle to identify whether something is a distraction or not because it feels too good to let go. This causes us into choose the distraction over God and, in turn, separates us from Him.

Flesh = Sarx (Greek): the flesh, denotes mere human nature, the earthly nature of man apart from divine influence, and therefore prone to sin and opposed to God

I am writing this in the hopes that after you read it, you get set free from the cloak of distraction—that distractions no longer have control over you but that you are able to stand up against them and become more spirit than flesh.

How to Identify a Distraction:

- It takes you away from God **(Exodus 20:1-3)**
- It gives your flesh temporary fulfillment **(1 Peter 1:23-25)**
- Getting rid of it seems impossible
- It contradicts the Word of God
- You want it/him/her more than you do God

How to Get Rid of a Distraction:

- Through prayer—a prayer that exposes distractions
- Reading the Bible because it brings truth and reveals what we

don't see

- Fasting—it allows the flesh to die and allows Holy Spirit to move **(Isaiah 58)**

- Be radical and remove it

How God Reveals the Distraction:

- The distraction becomes uncomfortable; you feel convicted

- Dreams and visions

- Through His word

- The distractions walk away

Why Does It Matter? Why Do I Need to Get Rid if Distractions?

No distraction leads to a life closer to God. Being closer to God leads to knowing Him. As a result, you hear His voice and know it's Him **(1 Corinthians 10:23-33)**.

When God begins to expose the distractions, do not fight it. Repent for allowing distractions to keep you away from Him and then move toward getting rid of them. There are consequences to our idolatry, whether we see them active in our lives now or in the future. Sometimes, we don't see them because they're affecting others instead of directly impacting us **(1 Corinthians 10:14-22)**.

For some of you, it may be your spouse. Surrender them to God. For some, it may be your children. Surrender them to God. Some of you, it may be food. Fast and pray for self-control. Some of you may be drawn to porn. Hide your devices at night and turn on worship as soon as the thoughts come in. Whatever it is, get rid of it!

Let Us Pray

God, I thank You for exposing the distractions in our lives. God, forgive us for putting distractions before You. We repent. Lord, we thank You for the Holy Spirit. May He take over and lead me to You. God thank You for giving me the wisdom and knowledge in this season to walk away from distractions. Be my strength as I say "no" to them today. God, I surrender the people I have allowed to be a distraction—those I have picked over You. God, I repent for making anyone an idol. In Jesus' name, Amen.

CHALLENGE FOR THE WEEK
Pray, worship, and read His word.

Chapter Six

Perseverance

Ooweee let's talk about it... I recently did a Bible study on the book of James and it was fireeeee. One of my main takeaways was *perseverance*. We hear all about the process, temptation, and trials. We are encouraged to keep pushing forward because there is something greater on the other side. But what is that greater thing on the other side?

Persevere: [verb] continue in a course of action even in the face of difficulty or with little or no prospect of success

Let's talk about the process... it can suck. But hold on, read this:

James 1:2-4 *"Consider it pure joy, my brothers and sisters, whenever you face trials of many kinds, because you know that the testing of your faith produces perseverance. Let perseverance finish its work so that you may be mature and complete, not lacking anything"* (NIV)

The testing of your faith produces perseverance. But wait... let perseverance finish its work so that you may be mature and complete! In other words, if we keep interrupting the testing of our faith, whether out of fear, weariness, anger, or whatever else, it will stop us from maturing and being complete in Him. Our walk is not meant to remain stagnant. We can not just accept Jesus as our Savior; we also have to apply the Lord (our Master) part. He is a better master than your flesh will ever be.

So What Is Faith?

Hebrews 11:1 *"Now faith is confidence in what we hope for and assurance about what we do not see."* (NIV) — Read the entire chapter to see faith in action.

Our confidence in what is hoped for and our assurance about what we do not see will be tested. Having the knowledge that you will be tested is both relieving and challenging to hear. Relieving because at least you know that it will happen. Challenging because we honestly don't want to go through it. But the scripture above tells us to "**consider it pure joy**." We know that joy comes from the Holy Spirit—it is a *fruit* of the Spirit **(Galatians 5:22)**.

Then it goes on to say that we will face trials of ***many kinds*** which means that the testing of our faith won't always look the same. The trial you faced in your last season will not look the same in your new season. But the following verses tell us to ask God for wisdom. Wisdom is what helps us know what to say yes or no to when facing trials (*the book of Proverbs is filled with wisdom*).

James 1:5 *"If any of you lacks wisdom, you should ask God, who gives generously to all without finding fault, and it will be given to you."* (NIV)

(So many nuggets about <u>doubt</u> in between these two verses. Go check it out!)

James 1:12 *"Blessed is the one who perseveres under trial because, having stood the test, that person will receive the crown of life that the Lord has promised to those who love him."* (NIV)

Blessed: [adjective] made holy; consecrated

BLESSED is the one who perseveres, having **STOOD** the test.... persevering makes us holy and consecrated. Not only persevering, but also standing firm in our faith. Standing. Our flesh is lazy, it lacks the motivation to persevere, and we gain nothing by giving in to it. But through persevering, we gain everything: the promise of God—eternal life.

HALLELUJAH, WE ARE BEING MADE HOLY UNTO GOD!! No longer will we run away from the test. Face it, stand firm, remember that we are blessed, and we will rejoice through the perseverance for His glory.

Let Us Pray

God, I thank You for giving us the wisdom to persevere. God, I thank You for warning us that the testing will come and for showing us the way through perseverance. God, I thank You that we will not get weary, but that through Your strength we will stand firm in our faith. God, You revealed to us through James that when we ask without doubt, we will receive. God, we thank You and honor You as Lord over our lives, in Jesus' name. Amen.

Chapter Seven

Insulting Grace

Recently, I studied Hebrews, and I experienced freedom. The hyper-fixation on grace in the Body of Christ has grieved me for a while now. I felt like people were abusing the grace of God. Using the excuse of God being gracious to continue living on their terms. It felt like a very dangerous way of preaching the gospel. It made me curious about how to preach the gospel without compromising, and God answered me as we were reading the text. It brought me so much clarity and confirmation about my grievance.

Hebrews 10:26-29 *"If we deliberately keep on sinning after we have received the knowledge of the truth, no sacrifice for sins is left, but only a fearful expectation of judgment and of raging fire that will consume the enemies of God. Anyone who rejected the law of Moses died without mercy on the testimony of two or three witnesses. How much more severely do you think someone deserves to be punished who has trampled the Son of God underfoot, who has treated as an unholy thing the blood of the covenant that sanctified them, and who has insulted the Spirit of grace?"* (NIV)

But wait... then I ran into this scripture...

Isaiah 26:10 *"But when grace is shown to the wicked, they do not learn righteousness; even in a land of uprightness they go on doing evil and do not regard the majesty of the Lord."* (NIV)

Yes, grace has been given to us, but do not be deceived into thinking you won it like a trophy you can flaunt. You did not pay the price; Jesus did. He sacrificed Himself so that we may live as new creatures. And to live as a new creature, we have to allow Him to do His work in us.

Grace: [noun] simple elegance or refinement of movement

Grace is powerful because it comes from Him, and through Him we are transformed. Grace will change you. It moves within you. Do not buy into the lie that because of grace, you can do whatever you want, because it simply is not true. Such teaching will lead you to insult the Spirit of Grace. It will make you wicked and unable to learn from grace. Grace transforms us. We understand that we do not deserve grace, but we lay our lives down for grace to do the works that we cannot do to please God.

2 Corinthians 12:9 *"But he said to me, "My grace is sufficient for you, for my power is made perfect in weakness.""*

We have to remember that anything that comes from Him is holy, and we are wicked. This means we are more susceptible to not wanting to do things the way God designed them to be. Study the Bible so that you may have a true understanding of His word and not just what your flesh wants to hear.

Let Us Pray

God, I thank You for Your grace. God, we bless Your name. We lift Your name on high. God, we repent for taking Your grace for granted and thinking that our way of living is better than Yours. Thank You for exposing our prideful nature and for forgiving us. God, thank You for being our strength. Thank You for transforming us. God, we do not deserve Your grace, but You made a way where there was no way. I thank You for convicting us God, so that we may continue being transformed in You. We love You, Lord, In Jesus' name. Amen.

CHALLENGE FOR THE WEEK

Reflect and see if you have been taking God's grace for granted. If you have, repent and direct your gaze back to God.

Chapter Eight
Stop The Search

Identity: [noun] the fact of being who or what a person or thing is

Why are we still searching for who we are? Why are we still identifying with our sins? What else do we need in order to receive an understanding of who we are?

When we are in the world, we are lost. But we have a desire to be found—even if it leads to all the wrong places. We fight for it. When we are focused on the world, we are so determined that this false identity we pick up is the right one for us. It doesn't matter how crazy we look or, even worse, that it leads us to death. And even when we are found and saved, we struggle to receive the truth. The truth about who we are and what it requires of us to remain in this place.

We get deceived into believing that we must take personality tests, follow horoscopes, or receive false ideologies to understand where we fit in. Just for educational purposes—because I want you all to see the truth for yourself—go research the root of personality tests and horoscopes. If it does not line up with the Bible, then we should not be following it. If the ideologies of your pastor, teacher, favorite influencer, or leader do not line up with His word, then we should not follow or accept them. When you desire truth, it will be given to you, and you will be set free.

Alright, let's take it a step further... As a Christian, you can no longer identify with being a part of the "BeyHive" or "Swifties" or any of your favorite singers/bands/artists. Why? Because your identity is not found in them. When you become a believer in Jesus Christ, you become a son/daughter of God. That is a promise.

John 1:12-13 *"Yet to all who did receive him, to those who believed in his name, he gave the right to become children of God—children born not of natural descent, nor of human decision or a husband's will, but born of God."* (NIV)

You have been reborn, my dear siblings. No longer can you search in the world for who you are. Stop the search. For you have been found. You have become a son/daughter of God. Now, what does that look like, you may ask? Go look at the true Son of God, Jesus. He is the perfect example to follow. If you struggle with your identity, search His word. Are you struggling to understand some of your quirks? Ask God and He will reveal. If God can save you from death, what more can He do?

Please beware of the things you identify with because many of those things are rooted in demonic activity. Identifying with those things will keep you in bondage. The reason the Israelites struggled for 40 years (besides murmuring and complaining) is that they forgot who saved them from bondage and, in turn, forgot who they were.

Psalm 106:21 *"They forgot the God who saved them, who had done great things in Egypt."* (NIV)

Why did God save? Because you belong to Him and a thief was trying to kill you, BUT FAILED.

Lastly, if we continue to seek our identity in the wrong things, it will lead us to the evil of self-seeking, which has severe consequences. Keep seeking in Him, not the world.

Romans 2:7-10 *"To those who by persistence in doing good seek glory, honor and immortality, he will give eternal life. But for those who are self-seeking and who reject the truth and follow evil, there will be wrath and anger. There will be trouble and distress for every human being who does evil: first for the Jew, then for the Gentile; but glory, honor and peace for everyone who does good: first for the Jew, then for the Gentile."* (NIV)

Let Us Pray

God, we repent for forgetting who we are and everything You have done for us. God, You didn't just find us; You saved us from death. We thank You, God, that we no longer have to keep searching because we have been found in You. God, reveal to us who we are to You. Lead us in Scripture—the truth. Dismantle every lie of the world. I no longer desire to believe the lies. God, I want the truth. I thank You in Jesus' name. Amen.

CHALLENGE FOR THE WEEK
Go research everything you follow, even if it has "Christian" in the title.
Ask God for discernment.

Chapter Nine
Who Can I Run To?

I hope you didn't start singing the song lol (but if you did, it's okay, I understand...). Have you ever met someone who goes by multiple names? Each name has a different back story or memory attached to it, but they're all used to call the same person.

I have a very difficult name to pronounce and it's hard to create any nicknames for it. When people pronounce it wrong, I don't overthink it because I know they are talking to me. There was a time when I went by a different name—Heidi. Because my teachers were having such a hard time pronouncing my name, their way of fixing it was by giving me a new name. I went by that name for 15 years of my life. When I gave my life to Christ, God began to deal with me about my name.

He revealed to me that that was not the name He had assigned to me. I didn't get what the big deal was, but I obeyed His instructions anyway. He told me to no longer identify with "Heidi" and to introduce myself as

Haydee (I-Day). After I did, I felt a weight come off of me. Shackles of confusion were broken off of me. I felt even my physical walk change. It's as if God called forth Haydee, the original creation, and activated her in that moment.

Haydee [meaning]: well-behaved; modest

Matthew 16:16-18 *"Simon Peter answered, "You are the Messiah, the Son of the living God." Jesus replied, "Blessed are you, Simon son of Jonah, for this was not revealed to you by flesh and blood, but by my Father in heaven. And I tell you that you are Peter, and on this rock I will build my church, and the gates of Hades will not overcome it."* (NIV)

I've noticed that God is very intentional about names. They're important to Him, which means they should be important to us. A name identifies us and tells us who we are to Him.

Did you know God has over 650 names?!

All of His names have a backstory and each name identifies a characteristic of God. It reminds of who He is, what He has done, and what He will continue to do.

God loves when we call Him by a specific name because that means we know Him for that characteristic now.

Example: You go by your birth-given name with acquaintances. But your family or close friends call you by your other names because they have gotten to KNOW you by those names and feel part of the backstories and memories. You know your acquaintances have become friends when a relationship has been built, and they feel comfortable enough to call you by those names.

When you build a relationship with God, you get to know Him by His other names: Provider, Healer, King, Ruler, God of war, God of justice, Comforter, etc. You know Him. God wants you to call Him by His name(s).

When you feel low and see no way out, call on God the Waymaker. When your enemies come against you, call on God the Defender. When you are experiencing sickness, call on God the Healer.

Be specific about who you are calling forth because He will arrive. If you have been desiring to grow in your prayer life or your relationship with God, get to know Him and call Him by the names that you have gotten to known Him to be.

CHALLENGE FOR THE WEEK

Look up the meaning of your name. Also, write down all the names you know God by so far.

Chapter Ten

Family

And the LORD passed by before him, and proclaimed, The LORD, The LORD God, merciful and gracious, longsuffering, and abundant in goodness and truth, keeping mercy for thousands, forgiving iniquity and transgression and sin, and that will by no means clear the guilty; visiting the iniquity of the fathers upon the children, and upon the children's children, unto the third and to the fourth generation.

– Exodus 34:6-7 (KJV)

I've spoken before about God calling family ministries to the forefront and generational curses. I want to dig a little deeper into what generational curses are and how they affect us now, as well as our future generations. The first time I ever heard about generational curses, I felt like my eyes were opened wide to the truth. It's like everything that I felt hindered me my whole life was exposed, and I was ready to put a stop to the curses that had been running in my family for years.

Curse: [noun] any expressed wish that some form of adversity or misfortune will befall or attach to one or more persons, a place, or an object.

Have you ever been compared to a family member or told that you act like Aunt Susie or Uncle Ron, whether good or bad? Have you noticed cycles of bad things happening within your family? For example, your great-great-grandfather died from cancer at the age of 30, and so did your great-grandfather, your grandfather, and unfortunately, your father did too. Another example is if all the women in your family struggle with anger. Curses can present themselves in a variety of natural forms that we may find normal but are actually deeply spiritual.

The problem with generational curses is that they've been normalized. If the enemy can get us to be ignorant or comfortable in these curses, then we will never be set free. Yes, we have been set free from the sacrifice of Jesus and our sins have been forgiven. But we must also continue to acknowledge that through His sacrifice, we have been given the Holy Spirit, AKA our advocate, AKA the Spirit of truth. If the enemy can keep you from acknowledging the power of the Holy Spirit that is within you, then he can keep you blinded from the truth. The truth is that generational curses are real, and you are most likely dealing with the consequences of your previous generations' actions, but the good news is that you can be set free!

The way to identify what those generational curses are and how they manifest through you or your family is by looking at some of the sins you struggle with and whether your family members also deal with those sins.

Sin: [noun] an immoral act considered to be a transgression against divine law.

Example 1: The women in my family always married or got involved with abusive men. Men who had anger issues and problems with addiction, which led to dysfunctional relationships. They would separate and get back together again and would drive the men to have children with other women. Growing up, I saw the dysfunction, and it turned me off from marriage, but it didn't stop me from being dysfunctional. I was abusive towards my girlfriend and played mind games with her. I wouldn't physically abuse her, but I played with her emotions, and I would separate from her and get back together with her to have control over her and the relationship. I also had issues with addiction.

If we dissect this pattern here, we see pride, perversion, sexual immorality, anger, addiction, adultery, lying, brokenness, and the destruction of the family structure God designed. The curses may not have manifested exactly the same with me, but the sins were still there. And they became curses because those sins stayed attached to me since I didn't start making changes once my sins were forgiven. Once you have received the Spirit of truth, you are enlightened to the ugliness in your life, and it is meant to be purified.

Example 2: The spirit of witchcraft is one sneaky spirit, and at the same time, it's so bold. There are some cultural things that people do that are essentially demonic rituals. But because of our ignorance and nostalgia, we just go with it. Burning sage to "clean/purify" the atmosphere, putting food out at a family member's grave for *dia de los muertos*, talking to ancestors, etc. Start to question everything you have been doing or celebrating out of habit or tradition. Look deeper and do research on the things you culturally celebrate. You may think it's innocent, but it could be inviting demonic entities into your family bloodline and keeping you and future generations in bondage.

Example 3: Health curses are real and they have been normalized by the medical industry because they make money from them. Can God use the medical industry to help us? Yes, absolutely. But in a lot of cases, we need to see the truth, and the truth is that the heart disease, gluttony, blood pressure issues, cancer, aneurysms, etc. that run in your family aren't just family health issues; they are generational curses that can end with you!

When you go for a doctor's visit, they give you a form to fill out. They ask you about the health problems that run in your family, and based on that information they have a better idea of what you are likely to deal with now or in the future. That's horrible! You're basically saying you have accepted the fate of dealing with diabetes or high blood pressure, and being on medication for the rest of your life. Generational curses can end, and they do not have to continue happening. They end with you acknowledging that they are there, denouncing them, and taking practical steps to create a new life for you and your future generations.

Canceling Generational Curses

Cancelling generational curses brings the future to life and opens the door for greater access for the future generations. We are stepping into a new era, and as you can see the demonic realm is becoming more and more bold every day. But God is bolder, and our children are being called to a higher place, spiritually.

However, in order for our children and their children to be set up to flow in the supernatural, we need to help them by paving the way and allowing the Holy Spirit to purify our bloodlines so we can become better disciples for our families. This is all for the glory of God. God gets the glory that I no longer struggle with my sexuality. God gets the glory that my family is no longer having children out of wedlock. God gets the glory that I no longer struggle with addiction to food, alcohol, and drugs. God gets the glory as I dedicate my family to serve Him for the rest of our days. Cancel generational curses by denouncing them in the name of Jesus. Some curses will end in that moment, and others you will have to practically unlearn as the Holy Spirit exposes them. But your Advocate is there to help you as you take those practical steps.

After I had my second child, I went through a season in which I felt physically unhealthy. I was at the heaviest weight I had ever been and I heard the Holy Spirit tell me that if I continued this unhealthy path, I would end up with diabetes. Diabetes ran on my mother's side of the family and it had affected the women on that side of the family (including my mother) for years. When I heard Him tell me this, I immediately repented and asked for the Holy Spirit to help me cancel the curse of diabetes. He helped me by changing my tastebuds and making me more aware of what I was taking in daily. I started working out and killing my flesh by teaching it discipline. After putting in the work for a while, I felt different—not just physically, but spiritually—and I heard the Holy Spirit tell me, "diabetes will no longer run in your family." I physically felt something break off of me and I rejoiced because my children would not have to deal with that curse and none of my future generations would either!

Identifying generational curses also protects you and your future generations from attacks. For example: If divorce runs in your family and you cancel that generational curse, then the enemy has no room to send a demonic assignment to bring separation to your marriage. Learn about your spouse's family and their generational curses because those will affect your children, and you will know how to intercede for your spouse and your kids.

If you want to learn more about generational curses, read the story of Abraham and Sarah, and that of Isaac and Rebekah, and dissect them to see the similarities

Let Us Pray

Lord, I thank You. I thank You for setting us free from generational curses. Thank You for the Holy Spirit, our Advocate, the Spirit of truth. Remove the veils off of our eyes, God. May we see clearly those curses that have been hiding in our families. I thank You for exposing us to the truth and setting us free. I thank You that those curses end with us. Thank You for teaching us new ways to live in freedom. God, I pray that every single chain is broken, in Jesus' name. Amen.

Chapter Eleven

Parents

This message is directed towards parents, but even if you're not a parent, it can still offer valuable insights on how to support the parents and children in your community. Building a generation devoted to God requires the collective effort of a caring community.

Here are a couple of questions I ask myself daily as my children watch me follow God:

Did they see God or did they see my flesh move in that conversation?

How can I represent You (God) as I lead them through this situation?

Our first year of parenthood was also our first year of marriage. It came with *so* many challenges. We almost gave up on our marriage and because of our struggles, we weren't able to be great parents to our daughter. Our son, on the other hand, was born into restoration. I quickly realized how we didn't give our firstborn 100 percent because of the spiritual attacks on our marriage. It broke us. We began to intercede for her, praying and declaring that none of the seeds that the enemy tried to plant would take root. We repented for not taking the assignment seriously and handed our daughter back over to God.

We realized that for us to teach our kids how to follow God, we have to be on fire for Him. The more on fire we got for Him, the more everything around us would catch fire. Our children have seen my husband and I in our ugliest moments with God. They have seen us question God. They have seen us be thankful for His mercy. They have seen when we struggle to pray. I refuse to show them only the 'good' parts of our walks. They see that our relationship with God isn't only based on the miracles He performs for us, but on how we surrender our lives daily to His will. We also don't want them to only see us on fire for God in the church building, but to know that this is the life we live.

They see Mom and Dad serve God outside of the church building through acts like serving one another, praying for strangers, and standing for truth. We do not sugarcoat things to our kids; we address when someone needs deliverance, we address the confusion, and we also point out that we are all in need of Jesus.

Parents, we have to stop living double lives and become what we desire our children to become in God: whole. We have allowed ourselves to become too common with our children without realizing that we need to honor the God in them. They are also Kingdom citizens and will not be children forever, but will become adult warriors of God. The way for the Kingdom to take over begins at home. This is why the enemy wants to destroy the family unit.

So, in closing, I leave you with this: Do your children see God, or did they see your flesh? How can you represent God better as you lead them?

Community, pray for the parents in your life and their children, that God may surround them with His presence, and for the discernment on how to lead them to Christ.

CHALLENGE FOR THE WEEK

Ask the Lord to reveal to you what changes you need to make as a parent to lead His children back to Him. Ask the Lord for conviction and repent.

Chapter Twelve
Return to your Lane

I heard this at an event recently, and it set me free. Sometimes, we can be in "routine mode" and not notice that we are being distracted—drifting into another lane—until it's too late. But by the grace of God, it was not too late for me, and it's not for you either.

Mature: [adjective] fully developed physically; full-grown

In some cases, the reason we do not mature is because we are so busy looking into other people's lanes that we get distracted and get off route. We try to figure out how they got into that position, why it took them a shorter time to get delivered, or why their lives look so perfect. But the reality is that trying to move into other lanes exposes us—the drivers. It exposes that something is going on within us.

As drivers, we are either not content with the route the GPS has us on, or we think the other lane is moving faster than ours. One of my pet peeves on the road is when there is that one driver who is in a hurry and does irrational things to get ahead. The driver puts not just themselves in danger, but the rest of the people on the road. I get nervous because at some point they will get humbled—either through road closure traffic, a red light, or even worse, an accident.

Sometimes, when you've been on the road for a long time and everything around you looks the same—just trees, open roads, and more trees—it feels like time begins to slow down and it makes the trip seem longer. But you don't realize that you've made a lot of progress and are getting closer to your destination. There are other times when you start getting bored and end up not paying attention to the road, which can cause you to drift out of your lane. It shakes you up a bit when you notice it happening, and you realize it's time for a break. That way, you can get back on the road fully aware and better equipped for an efficient ride.

I pray all of my examples are getting your reflection wheels turning. So now, let's apply these examples to our walks with God. I've done all of the above when it comes to my walk. I've gotten bored of the route He had me on and decided to try another one, only to realize my route was way longer. I decided to get on the lane that I thought would be faster for my career choices and quickly realized God's presence wasn't there. I've also been the reckless driver, not caring about how my choices affected those around me.

At a certain point, I have felt stalled in my walk, which led me to wonder about some of my peers' walks without realizing I was beginning to drift into their lanes. This was distracting me from my destination. All I see are trees around me, and it's beginning to feel too long. But I know I'm making progress. The road ahead of me is under construction. Once God is done, I'll have the go-ahead to drive on a smooth road again. Hearing ***"return to your lane"*** woke me up! It was like Holy Spirit was beeping at me to wake up.

In the same way, I just wanted to encourage you today to **RETURN TO YOUR LANE**! Do not allow the other drivers to distract you from your destination. The one that God, in His perfect will, has designed specifically for you! Let's allow the Lord to mature us and do His mighty work in us so that we may continue on the road, alert and attentive, as the drivers He would have us be.

Here are some scriptures to encourage you when you are tempted to drift or look at other lanes:

Hebrews 12:2-4 *"We must keep our eyes on Jesus, who leads us and makes our faith complete. He endured the shame of being nailed to a cross, because he knew later on he would be glad he did. Now he is seated at the right side of God's throne! So keep your mind on Jesus, who put up with many insults from sinners. Then you won't get discouraged and give up. None of you have yet been hurt in your battle against sin."* (CEV)

Romans 8:28 *"And we know that in all things God works for the good of those who love him, who have been called according to his purpose."* (NIV)

Matthew 6:33-34 *"But seek first his kingdom and his righteousness, and all these things will be given to you as well. Therefore do not worry about tomorrow, for tomorrow will worry about itself. Each day has enough trouble of its own."* (NIV)

CHALLENGE FOR THE WEEK

Reflect on whether or not you have been looking at other people's lanes.

Chapter Thirteen

Let's Stop Pretending

When people leave your presence, do they leave knowing that you live what you preach, or do they leave your presence confused? I have learned that I cannot control what other Christians do; I can only give my righteous judgment and leave it in the hands of God. But there is one thing I *can* control and that is how I choose to surrender my life to Christ.

When I first became a Christian, I surrounded myself with Christian content and listened to many sermons. I enjoyed learning from people when all of a sudden I started having dreams about the people I was listening to, and it was stuff that I couldn't understand. So, I asked the Holy Spirit to help me understand what was going on. He told me to *"pay close attention to the details."* God was exposing to me that some of the people I was listening to were not living the life they were preaching.

You know the saying, *"Do as I say, not as I do?"* Yeah, that's not meant for us to follow. This is what the Bible says:

James 1:22-25 *"Do not merely listen to the word, and so deceive yourselves. Do what it says. Anyone who listens to the word but does not do what it says is like someone who looks at his face in a mirror and, after looking at himself, goes away and immediately forgets what he looks like. But whoever looks intently into the perfect law that gives freedom, and continues in it—not forgetting what they have heard, but doing it—they will be blessed in what they do."* (NIV)

Once that information was exposed to me, I needed to decide whether I was going to accept freedom or not. I stopped listening to the people God exposed and began to pray for them. Because to preach something you don't follow is a dangerous place to be. You are living a lie, living in sin, and you are teaching others to live that way, too. **Let's stop pretending and start living what we preach.**

Ask God for discernment so that you may surround yourself with people who truly follow and teach the word of God. Ask God for conviction so that you may follow and do what His holy word says. There are a lot of wolves dressed in sheep's clothing that are being used to deceive generations with new, shiny things, great communication skills, and trying way too hard to be relatable.

If your favorite influencer, preacher, teacher, leader, etc., isn't directing you back to God then it's time to reconsider the infuence they have on your life. I love you, family. I am grieved by the deception, but I know that God will expose it if you are willing to receive the truth. **LET'S STOP PRETENDING AND TRULY SURRENDER OUR LIVES TO CHRIST.**

> **CHALLENGE FOR THE WEEK**
> Ask God for discernment and purge your surroundings.

Chapter Fourteen
Your Addiction Is Killing You

Have you ever heard people with addiction say, "I'm not an addict, I can stop whenever I want?" Um... the truth is, that's the lie that the enemy wants us believe—that we're in control and have the strength to stop whenever we're ready to walk away.

List of my addictions:

- Alcohol

- Weed

- Food

- Dysfunctional Relationships

- Attention

- Lying

- Pornography

- Masturbation

- Comparison

- Cycles of Self-Sabotage

God set me free from every one of those addictions because I didn't have the control or the strength to stop them myself. I had no idea that those addictions were leading me to death. When you encounter our holy God, it exposes the evil things residing in you. He exposes the lies you have been believing. He exposes our weakness and how we have nothing in control. The enemy makes us believe that we have all this power, but the truth is we have none. <u>HE</u> IS THE POWER.

I have seen God's power flow in my life. I saw how His conviction led me to quit all of it cold turkey. I saw how His truth softened my heart to say "yes" to His will. I saw His words transform me into a new creature.

Isaiah 6:1-8 *"In the year that King Uzziah died, I saw the Lord, high and exalted, seated on a throne; and the train of his robe filled the temple. Above him were seraphim, each with six wings: With two wings they covered their faces, with two they covered their feet, and with two they were flying. And they were calling to one another: "Holy, holy, holy is the Lord Almighty; the whole earth is full of his glory." At the sound of their voices the doorposts and thresholds shook and the temple was filled with smoke. "Woe to me!" I cried. "I am ruined! For I am a man of unclean lips, and I live among a people of unclean lips, and my eyes have seen the King, the Lord Almighty." Then one of the seraphim flew to me with a live coal in his hand, which he had taken with tongs from the altar. With it he touched my mouth and said, "See, this* *has touched your lips; your guilt is taken away and your sin atoned for." Then I heard the voice of the Lord saying, "Whom shall I send? And who will go for us?" And I said, "Here am I. Send me!""* (NIV)

Isaiah encountered a Holy God and recognized how unholy he was and it transformed him. It led him to answer the call. Your addictions are killing you. It's killing what God has placed inside of you. Acknowledge His presence in your life, surrender your will to Him. Acknowledge that you have a problem and need Him to set you free from the bondage of addiction. Your addiction is not greater than God. You've been addicted to dysfunctional relationships for far too long. You've been addicted to abuse for far too long It's time to be set free. You've been addicted to death row for far too long. It's time to come alive in Him.

Let Us Pray

God, only You are holy. Only You are worthy. Only You hold the power. God, set us free from the bondage of addiction in Jesus' name. Amen.

CHALLENGE FOR THE WEEK
Ask God to expose addictions in your life.

Chapter Fifteen

Sarah, Girl...

When you think about Sarah, you think about Abraham and the promise God made to them regarding their son. The Lord was keeping them in their waiting through a journey of faith before they had their son. But I would like to tell you how my view of Sarah changed.

I have been in the book of Genesis on and off since July. I have tried to be intentional about taking my time as I read the text. I decided to take every sermon I had heard (or interpretation of the text) out of my mind. I realized that after hearing a few sermons on the same topic, I wasn't going to go read the text for myself to see what was taught. This made me realize I had been blindly following man and leaning on other people's revelations.

I was craving a deeper place with God, which required me to stop reading the Bible based on hearsay. Instead, I had to read it from a place of knowing the truth because I sought the Lord. Okay, enough back story, lol; let's get into this wild journey of me seeing Sarah in a different light.

Sarah was messssyyyyyy.... When I tell you, I saw Sarah as this super sweet old woman who deserved all of God's promises for all the waiting she had to do. Sarah (still Sarai at the time) knew God was keeping her from getting pregnant (Genesis 16:2) but she still struggled with her insecurity of not being able to have children in her time, which led her to pimp out her servant, Hagar. I don't know why I thought Hagar was a willing participant, but she wasn't (Genesis 16:3). And then Sarah dared to get jealous that Hagar had a child. Then, got mad at Abraham and blamed him for her suffering. In a way, she was right because Abraham could have put a stop to this the moment she suggested it. It was like the Fall all over again.

And Sarah didn't stop there; she decided to abuse Hagar out of anger. Because of this, Hagar fled, but God met her and told her to return to Sarah. Not only did God give her hope and promise her that He would increase her descendants (Genesis 16:7-16), He made a covenant with Abraham and Sarah. God is a covenant-keeping God, and even though Abraham and Sarah made a mess, God was keeping His covenant regarding Abraham's seed.

Fast forward: Issac is born and Sarah is still insecure. Now she is offended by Ishmael's presence and how it would affect her son's inheritance (Genesis 21:8-10). So she tells Abraham to get rid of them... Messy. Abraham loves his son and is distressed about this, but God tells him to go forth with it and lets him know that He will take care of Ishmael. Dude, Sarah was problematic! But God made a covenant with her husband that their seed would bring forth our dear, beloved Jesus.

Sarah's insecurities led her to do messy things that affected people around her. She allowed her insecurities to do reckless things... BUT GOD. God met Hagar and Ishmael and took care of them. He was merciful. This wrecked me. For one, I saw God's hand moving even when people tried getting in the way, and I saw how messy we can be when we desperately desire something. We will get in our way even after knowing God's promises. I want to encourage you in this moment: GET OUT OF THE WAY. Get healed. Examine your heart. Open your eyes to see if you have affected anyone around you due to the fogginess of insecurities during the waiting season.

Insecurity: [noun] a state or feeling of anxiety, fear, or self-doubt

Do not allow any open door for the enemy to be able to use you due to anxiety, fear, or doubt. Find security in Jesus. He takes all anxiety, fear, or doubt when you lay it and surrender it before Him.

Psalm 55:22 *"Cast your cares on the LORD and he will sustain you; he will never let the righteous be shaken."* (NIV)

Matthew 11:28 *"Come to me, all you who are weary and burdened, and I will give you rest."* (NIV)

Let Us Pray

God, I have been Sarah before. I once allowed my insecurities to reign. God, I thank You for setting me free. I continue to surrender my will to Yours. God, I choose to continue trusting in Your promises. I choose You over anxiety, I choose You over fear, I choose You over doubt, I choose You every time, Father God. You are a covenant-keeping God, and that is where my hope comes from. I love You, oh good God. Thank You for exposing my heart, God. In Jesus name, Amen.

> **CHALLENGE FOR THE WEEK**
> READ THE BIBLE.

Chapter Sixteen

Letting Him Uproot

In the course of time Cain brought some of the fruits of the soil as an offering to the Lord. And Abel also brought an offering—fat portions from some of the firstborn of his flock. The Lord looked with favor on Abel and his offering, but on Cain and his offering he did not look with favor. So Cain was very angry, and his face was downcast. Then the Lord said to Cain, "Why are you angry? Why is your face downcast? If you do what is right, will you not be accepted? But if you do not do what is right, sin is crouching at your door; it desires to have you, but you must rule over it."

– Genesis 4: 3-7 (NIV)

When I first read this scripture, I felt bad for Cain. Like, this guy also brought an offering that the Lord did not receive. But I also felt conflicted by how quick he was to kill his brother, Able, after his offering was not accepted. People don't want to acknowledge this, but we are more like Cain than Able. We are bringing our offerings to God with the expectation that they will be received by the Lord. But unfortunately, your offering may not be pleasing to Him.

Let's dig into why Able's sacrifice was accepted, and Cain's was rejected.

Hebrews 11:4 *"By faith Abel brought God a better offering than Cain did. By faith he was commended as righteous, when God spoke well of his offerings. And by faith Abel still speaks, even though he is dead."* (NIV)

Hebrews 11:6 *"And without faith it is impossible to please God, <u>because anyone who comes to him must believe that he exists and that he rewards those who earnestly seek him.</u>"* (NIV)

Able's offering was brought by faith. Did Cain not believe in God? Why was Cain bringing an offering to God if he didn't believe in what God could do? What was in his heart that prevented him from bringing an offering by faith? His heart was exposed after his offering was rejected—it was full of anger. Sin was crouching at the door of Cain's heart and God warned him and told him he could rule over it. Now we know that the way to rule over sin is through God. But Cain was blinded by his sin, which gave the devil access to his heart.

Unfortunately, that is how some of us operate when God doesn't answer our prayers—we respond in ways that expose our hearts. It exposes how our hearts have always been: ratchet. We're quicker to give into sin than surrender to God.

Ephesians 4:26-27 *""In your anger do not sin" : Do not let the sun go down while you are still angry, and do not give the devil a foothold."* (NIV)

1 Corinthians 10:13 *"No temptation has overtaken you except what is common to mankind. And God is faithful; he will not let you be tempted be-*

yond what you can bear. But when you are tempted, he will also provide a way out so that you can endure it." (NIV)

God is looking at the offering you're bringing to Him. Is it out of faith or are you still in your sin? Are you fleeing from sin or are you letting it crouch at the door of your heart, waiting for you to give it access?

I used to relate to Cain. There was a time when I felt angry at God, like He wasn't hearing my prayers because I wasn't seeing them being answered. I was full of entitlement, and this opened the door to coveting. I began to covet the lives of my sisters in Christ, desiring their lives and thinking of ways that I could make things happen for myself. My heart was ratchet and my offerings of praise and worship were not pleasing to the Lord. I allowed sin to rule over me and it led me to sin against my Father.

Eventually, God opened my eyes. I saw how bitter I was and how quick I was to sin. I repented and decided that day that no matter what my life looked like, I would trust God and have faith in Him. I decided that I wanted my offering (my body, mind, and soul) to be a sweet fragrance to the Father. This is how we mature in Him by surrendering our wills to His.

Our God is so sweet. Even in our rebellious chaos He still hears us because He is present and everlasting. However, being with the Lord is not just about Him being there; it's about YOU being present with Him. You cannot be present with Him in that way if sin is crouching at your door. Become an offering pleasing to the Father.

Chapter Seventeen

This Is Your Reminder...

"Woman," Jesus replied, "believe me, a time is coming when you will worship the Father neither on this mountain nor in Jerusalem. You Samaritans worship what you do not know; we worship what we do know, for salvation is from the Jews. Yet a time is coming and has now come when the true worshipers will worship the Father in the Spirit and in truth, for they are the kind of worshipers the Father seeks. God is spirit, and his worshipers must worship in the Spirit and in truth."

– John 4:21-24 (NIV)

I used to be a very distracted worshipper; I constantly had something on my mind while worshipping—wondering if people could see me crying, wondering what other people looked like worshipping, nitpicking the worship songs that were being sung, and struggling with intrusive thoughts. I never felt safe just to let go and be free to worship. I would see people worshipping so freely that it made me wonder what I was missing.

I asked God, "What is preventing me from worshipping freely?" I realized I was making the worship about me and not about our holy God. I got too common with God and had no reverence or adoration for Him. It shouldn't be hard to worship my Savior, my Redeemer, the King of Kings!

I had to repent for my worshipping myself. Worshipping my thoughts instead of Him, worshipping my insecurities instead of Him, worshipping my fears instead of Him. I began to focus my worship on Him. I would have to cast down my thoughts, lay them down to Him, and continue worshipping. There had to be a renewing of my mind and Psalm 18 had to be written on the tablet of my heart.

Our desire should be to be **true worshippers**. Why? Because God is seeking them! **WHERE ARE THE TRUE WORSHIPPERS?**

Be intentional about worshipping our holy King every day. It shouldn't be hard. We shouldn't be so quick to forget what He saved us from. If you are reading this, that means you made it to see another day due to His mercy and grace. This should make you want to shout a "HALLELUJAH." Ask Him to make you sensitive to His presence. Ask Him to make you sensitive to His sound. Ask the Holy Spirit to give you songs to sing to the Lord. Remember that even the angels worship our God.

Isaiah 6:3 *"And they were calling to one another: "Holy, holy, holy is the Lord Almighty; the whole earth is full of his glory.""* (NIV)

Chapter 18
Broken Church System

All the believers were one in heart and mind. No one claimed that any of their possessions was their own, but they shared everything they had. With great power the apostles continued to testify to the resurrection of the Lord Jesus. And God's grace was so powerfully at work in them all that there were no needy persons among them. For from time to time those who owned land or houses sold them, brought the money from the sales and put it at the apostles' feet, and it was distributed to anyone who had need. Joseph, a Levite from Cyprus, whom the apostles called Barnabas (which means "son of encouragement"), sold a field he owned and brought the money and put it at the apostles' feet.

– Acts 4:32-37 (NIV)

We live in a time as believers in which we either fully know who we are in Christ, or we don't. We have a battle going on amongst ourselves because we are trying to fix a body that only Christ can fix. You have believers who are "deconstructing" their faith because of man, not because of Jesus. You have believers running after other believers, babysitting them instead of focusing on those who are not in the Kingdom who truly need a home. Many are still trying to figure out where they stand with the Lord because they have commitment issues and do not commit to God in the way that He desires them to. We also have believers who are more mature in the things of God who have moved beyond the earth realm into to the realm where God has revealed mysteries to them. But instead of yearning and learning from them, many people condemn them for being too outside the box.

When I was reading the book of Acts, I saw a church that was powerful because they were operating from one heart and one mind. Believing in the name of Jesus and receiving the gift of the Holy Spirit united them in prayer, which united them in power. The Gospel was able to spread, and people joining the Body was being multiplied!

I fled from the church system because I was tired of seeing the "same old, same old" with no evidence of the power of the Holy Spirit. I got tired of hearing prophecy because it came with some money scam afterward. I was tired of hurt leadership portraying their hurt on their congregation. I was tired of church members not experiencing true change because they didn't have the faith to allow Jesus to change them. Most of all, I was tired of all the cliques. I just wanted Jesus.

But my prayer has to change. I just want to flow from the power of the Holy Spirit. Even though that's already my prayer, I mean it from the point of view of not even looking to the sides but keeping my eyes forward. Praying that others will also join with one heart and one mind. Then the evidence of the Holy Spirit will do the rest.

Being One Body

The key here is that the church has been operating as a system and not as a body.

__System: [noun] a set of things working together as parts of a mechanism or an interconnecting network; a set of principles or__ *procedures according to which something is done; an organized framework or method.*

Body: [noun] the physical structure of a person or an animal, including the bones, flesh, and organs

I do not want to be apart of a system where there is no life and there are just procedures. I want to be apart of a body that is alive. Yes, we are some flawed individuals but we should all be carrying one mission—regardless of what arena God has called us to—and that is to share the Good News to everyone we can reach.

The Good News is what brought us all here, and that's what's going to keep us going. If you want to know what your purpose is in this body, it's simple: Share the Good News! It's time to stop overanalyzing our purpose on this earth. It's time for us to wake up and share! If you left the church building because of man, I have bad news for you... you never left the church. You are a part of this church body.

Let Us Pray

Lord, I thank You for the Body. I thank You that You are our hope. God, forgive us for allowing Your body to become a system. God, revive us. Place a boldness in us to share Your good news. Give us compassion to see beyond ourselves. May the power of the Holy Spirit flow through us and produce the fire that this cold world needs. God, I thank You for saving us. In Jesus' name, Amen.

Afterword

I pray that as you read this book, you experienced the conviction of the Holy Spirit and that your mind was transformed and renewed in Him. I pray that you became even more dependent on Him. I pray His words penetrated your heart and that they soothed any pain or trauma through His healing power. I pray that as you reflect on each chapter, you grow deeper in Him.

Our only goal as believers should be to direct each other back to the only Source—to encourage one another to read His word because that is where true freedom comes from. The next and final section is a tool that I believe will help you grow deeper in His word—a student of the Holy word.

I have been using this study method since I got saved, but at the time, I didn't realize I was using a method; I just wanted to know God's word. In 2022, I realized that I needed to grow deeper in His word, not just from a student's perspective, but as a daughter getting to know her Father's perspective. God wanted me to engage more and to be curious about His word. I went back to my Bible study method but added a Q&A section. More specifically, I would ask God questions by faith, believing that He would answer at some point... and He did! Having childlike faith brought me closer to Him.

In 2024, God wanted me to look into the concept of photosynthesis and match it to my Bible study method, and it blew my mind. It took my understanding of His word to a new level. The Photosynthesis Bible Study Template was created to help you study His word by using the growth of a plant as an analogy. Each step opens a dialogue with God and brings you closer to Him. I encourage you to take your time with each stage and learn to fall in love with Him through His word.

Photosynthesis

Bible Study Template

Photosynthesis is a biological process many cellular organisms use to convert light energy into chemical energy, which is stored in organic compounds that can later be metabolized through cellular respiration to fuel the organism's activities.

This resource uses the photosynthesis process as an analogy to study God's word. This template is designed to bring you closer to God through studying His word and asking questions through the photosynthesis analogy. As you answer these questions it'll open a dialogue with God and create a space to develop a relationship with Him. This is not a self-centered Bible study template; it is God-centered.

Seeds

Write down what seeds were sown into you through the scripture.

Tip: Pray before getting in His word. My go-to prayer is "I'm here, Holy Spirit. Speak."

Water

What other Scriptures can you use to water the seeds?

Light

What is the Holy Spirit exposing within you through the scripture?

Weeds

WHAT WEEDS NEED TO BE UPROOTED IN YOUR LIFE?

Bloom

How can you apply everything that you've learned today in your growth with God?

Tip: Praise and thank Him as you are reading His word.

The Gardener

What does the scripture reveal about The Gardener (God)?

Tip: It's important for us to see God through His word. Reading the word is not always about us.

Bictionary

Write down any names or words that intrigued you and write their definitions.

Tip: The BLB app is a great tool for this.

Prayer and Repentance

This is where you take your time to pray, repent, and break any old covenants.

Tip: Do not be afraid of the Holy Spirit exposing you. Deliverance is good.

Q&A

God loves our curiousity. Ask God questions with faith the size of a mustard seed and believe that He will answer in His timing.

About the Author

EMPOWERING WOMEN THROUGH FAITH AND BEAUTY

Haydee Irving, a prominent social media influencer and the creative force behind Haydee Cosmetics, is a true visionary in the world of beauty and empowerment. Born with a deep passion for the things of God, motherhood, and truth, Haydee has dedicated her life to inspiring women to embrace their inner beauty and activate their creativity, all while finding strength in their identity in Christ.

As the founder of Haydee Cosmetics, a unique makeup brand centered around Christian values, Haydee has redefined the beauty industry by merging faith and beauty. Her brand not only provides high-quality cosmetics but also serves as a platform for empowering women to recognize their worth and potential in God.

What sets Haydee apart is her commitment to spreading the message of Christ's love and liberation. She firmly believes in the transformative power of faith and shares her journey of deliverance from the LGBT lifestyle through a supernatural encounter with God. This personal testimony adds a profound layer to her brand, inspiring others to seek truth and embrace the freedom found in their relationship with God.

Haydee's online presence as a social media influencer has allowed her to reach a vast audience, sharia rofound messages of faith and empowerment. Her authenticity, coupled with her unwavering dedication to Christ, has created a community of women who are not only beautiful on the outside but also strengthened by their faith from within.

In her pursuit of truth and passion for the things of God, Haydee continues to impact lives, encouraging women to embrace their unique beauty, activate their creativity, and, most importantly, find freedom and purpose in their identities in Christ.

To learn more about Haydee, please visit:
www.haydeeirving.com
www.haydeecosmetics.com

www.ingramcontent.com/pod-product-compliance
Lightning Source LLC
LaVergne TN
LVHW041712060526
838201LV00043B/703